The Essence Of
Organic Gardening

SEEING AND DOING THINGS DIFFERENTLY

A Practical and Inspirational Handbook for
Ecologically Conscious Gardeners

By Heide Hermary

Illustrated by Christina Nikolic

Gaia College
"Cultivating Community"

The Essence of Organic Gardening
Seeing and Doing Things Differently
First Edition

Library and Archives Canada Cataloguing in Publication

Hermary, Heide, 1948 –
The Essence of Organic Gardening: Seeing and Doing Things Differently: A Practical and Inspirational Handbook for Ecologically Conscious Gardeners /
by Heide Hermary; illustrated by Christina Nikolic

Includes bibliographical references
ISBN 978-0-9735687-4-5

1. Organic gardening
I. Nikolic, Christina, 1969 - II. Title.

SB453.5.H463 2008   635\'.0484
C2008-903715-4

Cover design: Sonja Callaghan
Photo of Heide Hermary: Michael Hermary
Gaia College logo: Peter Allen

Gaia College
"Cultivating Community"

Publisher:
Gaia College Inc., 2485 Koksilah Rd., Cowichan Station, B.C. V9L 6M7, Canada
www.gaiacollege.ca
E-mail: info@gaiacollege.ca

This book is dedicated to the volunteers
of the Society for Organic Urban Land Care.

You are an inspiration to all of us.

About Gaia College

Gaia College
"Cultivating Community"

Gaia College was established to meet the growing need for practitioners of environmentally sound horticulture. The college works in partnership with professional associations, public educational institutions, community organizations and private corporations.

The Gaia College Mission

- To teach a conscious way of living and working with nature
- To facilitate holistic thinking and practices through integration of knowledge from many disciplines
- To promote and demonstrate stewardship and regeneration of local and global resources
- To promote and demonstrate principles of conserving and regenerating biodiversity
- To provide a cooperative environment for the expression of ideas and interchange of knowledge
- To be motivated by love and service, not fear and greed.

Thank you!

Thank you to our instructors and students who generously shared their experiences in the garden, field and classroom. Thank you for the questions I couldn't answer, which forced me to learn more. Thank you to all who reviewed various drafts of this book, particularly Lisa Atkins, Sonja Callaghan, Dayle Cosway, Laurie Hardy, Michael Kim, Phil Nauta, Christina Nikolic, Beate Shanahan-Clarke, Jutta Vayas, and my husband Michael Hermary. Your suggestions were invaluable. Thank you to the many scientists and authors whose brilliant work increased my own understanding of natural processes, and who provided the scientific foundation for this book. And thank you to my husband, children and grandchildren and my dear aunt Gisa for your unwavering love and support.

Heide Hermary

When we know that – we too – are part of Nature,

we will take care of the Earth

Contents

Why I wrote this book

Many years ago, when I studied landscaping, I learned that the garden was an outdoor room, filled with structural elements arranged in an aesthetically pleasing fashion. Plants were selected for their shape, colour and texture, all neatly arranged like sofa cushions, to be kept tidy and under control so as not to spoil the perfection.

The need for tidiness spilled over into garden maintenance. The fallen, naturally recycling leaves and branches were considered "debris" and "litter", to be removed instantly to keep the soil surface clean. Even the plants were to be pruned and sprayed and dusted to remove all blemishes and plant feeding insects.

Over time - as I gained a deeper understanding of the connectedness of life on our planet - I came to see things very differently. It transformed the way I look at the world, and the way I garden - and it fills me with hope for the future.

I can now see that the garden's purpose is much greater than our pleasure, and that gardening is much more important than I thought.

The sofa cushion garden

And I also came to see that gardening is much simpler than I thought, requiring no special skills - just a little shift in the way we think about our garden. With this book I hope to show you a glimpse of the real beauty of the garden - a beauty that transcends the shapes and colours and the perfect spatial arrangement of objects. Beyond the obvious, below the surface, deep within the hidden places of the garden - that's where you will see a perfection and elegance that surpasses all imagination.

And I hope that - by seeing different things - you too will gain a different understanding of life and your role as a gardener. More importantly, may it inspire you to do things differently.

Enjoy!

Heide Hermary
Cowichan Station, B.C.
May, 2008

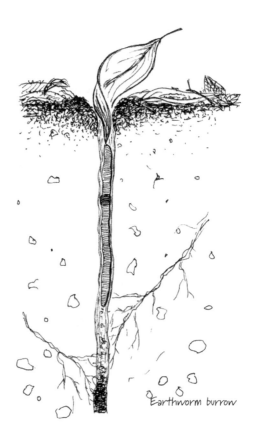

Earthworm burrow

Part One

Seeing Things Differently

It seems natural to focus on the biggest inhabitants of the garden and to think that gardening is all about plants. But it is so much more.

The garden is a highly ordered world that extends from the top of the tallest tree deep into the earth. It is a community of countless living organisms, all working hard to build their homes, feed themselves and raise their offspring.

While we focus on the plants - and perhaps the birds and butterflies - most of the species inhabiting the garden live in the soil and are so small that they can only be seen with the most powerful microscope. Yet their relationships are every bit as complex as ours.

Every species has a unique set of tasks and every individual makes a contribution towards the benefit of the whole. When we look closely, we can see an intricate web of relationships, alliances and even cooperatives that rival our human institutions in sophistication.

The foundation of life

Let's begin by taking a giant step back to the time when primitive organisms came together to form the relationships that would become the foundation of life on earth. Life as we know it would not exist without the cooperation of two very unlikely partners - plants and bacteria.

All of the carbohydrates in our food and in every cell of every living being, and all the carbon in the soil used to be part of the air - carbon dioxide (CO_2). It is the unique task of plants, algae and certain kinds of bacteria to extract the carbon from the carbon dioxide and incorporate it into solid compounds. This is what we call photosynthesis.

But that's only half of it. Photosynthesis is only possible through the activity of proteins, enzymes and similar substances in plant cells. One of the major building blocks of these molecules is nitrogen. Nitrogen also occurs naturally as a part of air - and even though plants are able to capture carbon dioxide gas they cannot capture nitrogen gas. This is the job of the nitrogen fixing bacteria, who are able to convert nitrogen gas into solid form. Ultimately, all the protein in our food and in the bodies of all living organisms has its origin in the work of these tiny creatures. But just like us, they totally depend on plants and recycled organic matter for their carbohydrates.

Clover with nitrogen fixing bacteria in roots

These bacteria live in the soil, on plant surfaces, and some even live right inside plant roots and leaves where they trade their nitrogen directly with the plant in exchange for sugars. Neither can exist without the other, and none of us would be here without their cooperation. The creation of life on earth is truly a group effort.

In Mother Nature's garden abundance continually increases, as ever more carbohydrates and proteins are created. The greatest biodiversity on land is found in the top few inches of the soil, where these basic building blocks of life are constantly recycled as one organism's waste becomes another's food. The end product, the most highly refined waste, is humus, which - in these times of climate change - we cherish for its ability to moderate the CO_2 content of the atmosphere. But the carbon doesn't get into the soil without the work of plants and the whole complex soil based web of life.

All of this comes to a halt when we - with our obsession with tidiness - deprive the soil dwelling organisms of their primary carbohydrate source: the old and discarded plant parts.

The community of the garden

Thistle and bee

We often think of Nature in adversarial terms - as a struggle for survival of the fittest - but the garden teaches us that "fitness" includes the ability to cooperate with others.

For instance, as primary carbohydrate producers it is the ecological destiny of plants to be eaten - and yet they flourish! That is because they have entered into relationships with many other organisms to obtain help with food procurement, defense and even procreation. In fact plants actively trade up to 80% of all the carbohydrates they produce through photosynthesis for the services of other organisms in their environment.

Everybody knows about pollinating insects such as bees and beetles, and even birds and bats, but how many of us realize that thousands of plant species have effectively contracted these animals to facilitate their entire sexual propagation! For these services plants trade primarily nectar and pollen, substances custom manufactured to meet the specific needs of their pollinators.

The nutrient requirements of some pollinators, such as ladybugs and lacewings, are more complex. Their young ones are meat eaters, feeding exclusively on small, soft-bodied insects such as aphids. And so the plants are content to host a few aphid colonies on their buds or leaves to create breeding grounds for their pollinators - just enough to meet the needs of the ladybugs, not enough to hurt the plants.

12

Homes in the soil

Soil dwelling organisms use and rearrange the raw materials in their environment to construct their homes - and they are not all that different from ours. With their excretions microbes glue the sand, silt and clay particles of the soil together to create chambers: large chambers for air, smaller chambers to store water, and space enough for their populations to flourish.

Gardeners spend millions of dollars each year to mechanically aerate their lawns because the soil has become so compact that grass roots don't have enough air. But the aerator is the wrong tool - what the lawn really needs is microbial diversity. As the microbes rearrange the soil particles to build themselves homes, they also create the ideal mix of soil pores to provide sufficient air for themselves and for plant roots. In a healthy lawn, repeated aerating is actually counterproductive, as it constantly destroys what the microbes have worked so hard to create.

Of all the ecosystems, healthy, biodiverse grasslands are the most effective in building topsoil and accumulating carbon in the soil. This is something to consider, as we are concerned about the climatic effect of carbon emissions.

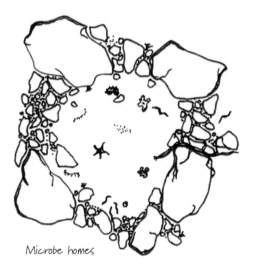

Microbe homes

The connectedness of life

We are often told that plants manufacture *all* their own carbohydrates, or that they *only* take up nutrients in their ionic (chemical) form or that the nutrients *must* be dissolved in water, but plants have many sources for everything they need.

Many of these misconceptions arise from the erroneous interpretation of scientific experiments. We cannot learn about a plant's natural behaviour from growing it in an unnatural, sterile environment, subjecting it to unusual treatments, and finally dissecting its remains. Plants are an extension - an inseparable part of - their environment.

Science likes to reduce everything to a single variable, but life is not like that, and plants are not mere mechanical contraptions. Everything has more than one cause and more than one effect - the natural environment is a complex, interrelated and connected web of life. The lives of plants, animals and microbes are so closely entwined that it's impossible to know where one ends and another starts.

A single change, a single introduction of a foreign substance has far reaching effects. Many decades later we begin to see the disastrous environmental effects of pesticide use, or the climatic effects of clear-cutting our forests.

Organic gardeners seek to create and maintain healthy, biodiverse ecosystems, because ecosystem health and plant health go hand-in-hand. In this way organic gardening supports the ecological roles of plants and their allies - the formation of organic molecules, the very foundation of life.

Organic gardening is not about substituting toxic chemicals with less toxic ones, but about a whole different way of thinking and working. It is a conscious effort to cooperate with Nature in the creation of health and abundance for all.

In the human economy we call this "outsourcing", but for the plants and their pollinators these arrangements have life or death consequences because there are no alternatives, no "opt-out" clauses. Without pollinators many plant species will simply die out, and without a diverse plant population providing year-round food the pollinators cannot survive. The greater the diversity, the greater the safety margin.

Other relationships are more difficult to see because they take place below ground. Half the plant lives in the soil, which not only anchors the plant, but is also its source of nutrients and water. Like us, plants can't live on carbohydrates alone, but require a balanced diet - and that can be challenging, being stuck in one place!

For example, many nutrients - especially phosphorus and some micronutrients - exist in rock formations that are difficult for plants to dissolve, and so plants have engaged the services of special types of fungi. These fungi, called

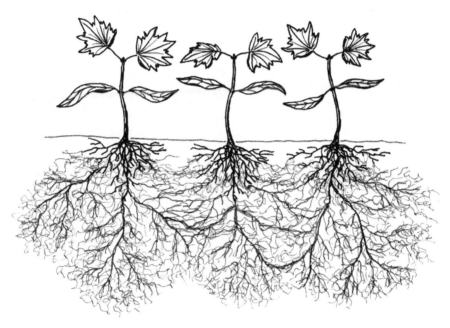

Mycorrhizal fungi connecting plant roots

mycorrhizal fungi, anchor themselves in plant roots and from there extend their long strands of mycelium into the surrounding soil. Their powerful digestive enzymes break down these rocks to harvest the nutrients, which they then trade with the plants in exchange for carbohydrates.

Mycorrhizal fungi also assist the plant with water uptake. The fungal network increases the root area - the water absorption area - of the plant many times, and so effectively renders the plant more "drought tolerant". In addition, the dense fungal strands act as the root's first line of defense in a world teeming with microbes. Some species of mycorrhizal fungi literally wrap themselves around the roots, completely protecting them from potential predators.

A single plant associates with many different species of these fungi, and each fungus associates with many different species of plants, so all plants in the garden are actually physically connected via the fungal network. And here we find that mycorrhizal fungi also work as messengers between plants, even transferring nutrients from one plant to another. So a healthy garden becomes like a single organism, acting in unison, a life form in its own right.

The relationships between plants and nitrogen fixing bacteria, and plants and mycorrhizal fungi, are only two examples of the many trade agreements plants have with other organisms in the soil. The area in the immediate vicinity of plant roots is alive with thousands of species, which feed on the carbon compounds excreted by plants and in turn produce substances that the plants

Soil biodiversity

require, such as vitamins, amino acids, enzymes and growth hormones. Plants may be able to photosynthesize, but they also absorb a significant amount of "processed" organic carbon from the soil. Sometimes it's cheaper to bring in pre-assembled parts than to manufacture everything from scratch - a concept we are well familiar with in our human economy.

The countless organisms in Nature - and in our garden - thrive because they make a valuable contribution to the whole. We have only just begun to understand the complexity of this interconnected web of life. It would serve us well to recognize the inherent intelligence in Nature, and to work with it rather than trying to subject it to our limited imagination.

The concept of health

Ecosystems are composed of organisms with complementary needs, including light, air, space, water and nutrients. Every species occupies a slightly different ecological niche, prefers different foods, and in turn contributes different value-added products towards someone else's food supply. The greater the biodiversity, the greater the overall fertility of the soil and the chances that all will find exactly what they require for optimal health.

We are what we eat, and the same is true for plants and all the other organisms in the garden. Just like us, plants, animals and microbes cannot thrive without balanced nutrition. We derive our food from the plants, the plants derive their food from the air and the soil.

We like to think that plant feeding insects and microbes - what we call "pests and diseases" - are the cause of our plants' problems, but they are only the result.

Insects perceive their environment with their antennae. Just like man-made antennae, they are tuned to receive one or more electromagnetic frequencies. For instance, when the female moth's pheromones attach themselves to the male moth's antenna, the insect decodes their frequency and interprets it as "mate".

Moth

Plants also emit many volatile substances, and only when a plant's vibrational frequency enters the range a plant predator ("pest" or "disease organism") equates with "food", will it be attracted to and feed on that plant. And that only happens when a plant is deficient in one or more nutrients. A healthy plant is - for all practical purposes - invisible to its predators.

Killing the "pests" does not change anything, as no amount of pesticides can provide the plant with the nutrients and growing conditions it requires. We can clearly see this in agriculture where year after year ever more potent pesticides are applied because we are forever treating the symptom, not the cause.

The cause of plant disease is poor nutrition and an unhealthy soil ecosystem. The fate of plants is as inseparably entwined with that of the soil as our fate is entwined with theirs. If we want to eat nutritious food we need to take care of the soil, for we too are part of this web of life. We think we protect our plants by killing the plant-feeding insects and microbes, when in fact they remove only the weak and diseased, and keep plant species strong. Instead we should thank the insects for removing the nutrient deficient plants from our own food supply.

But what about weeds? Weeds are nothing more than plants that are better adapted to the growing conditions our garden provides than the plants we would rather see. The ability of a plant community to adapt to changing

Beneficial insects

In Mother Nature's eyes all insects are created equal. Gardeners generally consider insects to be beneficial when they prey on plant "pests". For instance ladybugs and their larvae eat aphids, and so in our eyes ladybugs are beneficial, aphids are not.

These sentiments arise from a misunderstanding of natural processes. A healthy plant may be nibbled on, but it will not be infested with insects or microbes. These only seriously attack nutrient deficient plants, and within an ecological context that is highly beneficial - to the plant species that remain strong, and also to the species that depend on the healthy plant as food, such as larger animals and humans.

When we import predaceous insects in response to a "pest" problem we actually use them as a pesticide. When their food source is exhausted they will either die or move on.

In a healthy, biodiverse garden it should never be necessary to import "beneficial" insects, because their populations will already be established. This also means that we need to tolerate a few "pests", because without them their predators would have no food. The greater the plant diversity, the greater the insect diversity - and that is beneficial to the ecosystem as a whole.

Aphids and ladybugs

environmental conditions is Nature's intelligence at work. When one species suffers another takes its place, and the greater the diversity the more resilient the ecosystem is as a whole. But when our lawn suffers and its helpful companion plants fill in and ensure a continuous food supply for the soil dwelling organisms we call them weeds and kill them. However, no amount of herbicides can provide the grass with the growing conditions and nutrients it requires.

A healthy ecosystem has the resilience to deal with adversity. Populations of individual species fluctuate through drought years and floods, excessive heat and cold, but the great diversity of species allows the community as a whole to retain its overall cohesion.

The loss of biodiversity on our planet is very troubling at this time of global climate change. We need to protect what remains, and to re-establish plants and soil health in the areas already depleted.

Biodiversity

Time to do things differently

In our ignorance we gardeners have taken ourselves rather seriously. We thought it our job to feed our plants, and to protect them from their predators and as a result - unaware of the elegance of the web of life - destroyed the soil ecosystem with toxic chemicals. We thought we could improve on Nature and create order out of chaos. But Nature is already ordered and perfect, and plants already know how to take care of themselves.

In ignorance - and some say arrogance - the human species has devastated the planet's natural vegetation and soils - its life support systems - to the point of possible self-destruction.

It is even more humbling to realize that on our own we are powerless to repair what we have destroyed. It is not our task on this planet to capture carbon and nitrogen from the air, and gather the minerals from the soil and turn them into organic form. That is the domain of the plants and the soil-based web of life. At best we can support them, to help them do their jobs as efficiently as possible.

Part Two

Doing Things Differently

How can we help?

To start with, we need to do a lot less.

We need to stop treating the garden as if it were a room needing decoration. We need to stop injuring our plants by cutting them into shapes that please us. We need to stop killing - stop poisoning the soil and waterways and air, stop poisoning the insects and plants themselves.

We need to consciously think and work differently. Organic gardeners are not governed by maintenance schedules and social conventions. Instead each of our actions is evaluated for its effectiveness in supporting plants, animals and microbes to perform their ecological function. Our role in the garden is to ensure optimal ecosystem health.

This is easy when we think of gardening in terms of
- creating communities,
- feeding the soil dwelling organisms,
- increasing microbial diversity, and
- ensuring sufficient water for ecosystem health.

For sources of products mentioned in this section, please refer to the resources page at the end of the book.

Ladybug life cycle

Creating communities

Companion planting

In Nature plants always live in communities with many other plants, forming complementary relationships with respect to light exposure, root depth, nutrient and water requirements, and so on.

This is easy to see in forests, where the large trees are exposed to full sun, but the under-storey plants live in shade. Photosynthesis is powered by solar energy, and plant leaves are living solar collectors, finely tuned to specific light intensities. Depending on their adaptation to ultraviolet light, leaves also contain different levels of natural sunscreens. When we design and plant our gardens it is very important to provide plants with the light conditions they require. The sensitive leaves of shade plants will burn in full sun, and sun plants are not able to get sufficient light for photosynthesis when placed in shade.

Complementary root systems

Pruning

Trees do not need pruning. They already know how to engineer their structures to fortify themselves against prevailing winds and capture the best available light. The tree carefully balances the size and form of its trunk and branches with the size and extent of its root system. This is important for its structural integrity - but it's equally important to preserve the fine balance between the canopy's capacity to photosynthesize, and the root system's capacity to absorb nutrients and water from the soil. Whenever a tree is pruned, its roots die in corresponding proportion.

Pruning is a deliberate injury, weakening the tree and creating raw wounds that are unprotected against insect and microbe attacks. We are often told that pruning is an effective method to protect our trees from pests and diseases - how can we possibly assume this is helpful to a tree that is already under stress? With appropriate nutrition and growing conditions trees already know how to protect themselves, and they do not need our interference. It is time we learned to respect the intelligence in Nature. Trees thrived long before the evolution of the human species, and will likely continue to thrive long after we are gone.

In almost all situations the "need" to prune arises from inappropriate plant choices. Trees require a lot of space, above and below ground. That beautiful little tree in the five gallon container may in time grow a canopy spanning thirty feet or more!

Our job is to create and maintain healthy ecosystems, and that includes preventing predictable problems. Pruning can almost always be prevented through appropriate plant choices. Where pruning is unavoidable, please hire an arborist with extensive advanced training in tree health care.

Prairie plants, such as grasses, have adapted to grow in full sun. It makes little sense to expect grasses to flourish in the shade of trees - and they don't, and so we should be thankful to the mosses when they fill in the bare spots and ensure a continued carbohydrate supply for the soil organisms.

We commonly associate companion planting with vegetable gardens, because experience has taught us that some plants "get along" well with each other, and others don't. For instance, tomatoes grow well with carrots, lettuce and rosemary, but not with potatoes, cabbage and fennel. The same principle applies to all plants. Those that have evolved within the same ecosystem are used to each other's chemistry and other peculiarities and know how to live together.

Compatibility cannot be guaranteed when we group plants from many parts of the world in our ornamental gardens, even when we have taken the greatest care to provide them with the right growing conditions. It is generally easier to emulate native ecosystems, because the plants are so fully adapted to each other.

Of course our gardens can be aesthetically pleasing! We just need to be a bit more thoughtful in our plant choices and plant placement, and always remember that we are working with ecosystems.

Providing food and habitat

Ecosystems are composed of more than just plants. Animals, fungi, bacteria and other microscopic creatures are equally important participants, and all require year-round food and shelter.

Pollinating insects, for instance, need nectar - flowering plants - from spring to fall. But that is not enough - insects are very complex creatures and go through many changes during their short life. Caterpillars - butterfly larvae - look nothing like the adults, and require totally different food. We don't like it when they eat the leaves of our plants, but Nature operates on a very large scale and we need to look beyond our own comfort zone.

Butterfly life cycle

Many of the garden's inhabitants over-winter in the litter layer, freshly provided by the plant community as it sheds its leaves for the winter. When we clean up our garden in the fall we do untold damage to thousands of animal populations including our native predaceous insects. In the spring we complain about aphids on our plants, yet in the fall we've killed their natural predators by raking up the leaves and depriving them of safe winter habitat.

Winter is a difficult time for many of our garden's animals that require food or an undisturbed place to hibernate. Gardens that provide a diversity of nuts, berries and seeds become havens for birds that in turn will reduce insect populations in the summer.

When we take time to observe we can see that everything is connected. Plants cannot exist on their own, but require the support of microbes, animals and even other plants in their environment. The greater the diversity above ground, the greater the health and biodiversity in the soil. And of course the healthier the soil, the healthier the plants: biodiversity and health go hand-in-hand.

Our role is to provide plants with their natural companions, above ground and also in the soil. We need to learn to create ecosystems rather than plant collections. And we need to allow our plants the opportunity to form the relationships that sustain them.

Feeding the soil dwelling organisms

Mulching

Nature's soil management program starts with mulching. Old leaves and other discarded plant parts are simply deposited on the soil surface, where they provide food and habitat for the soil dwellers. What we call decay is actually the feeding activity of countless animals and microbes, most of which are too small to see without the most powerful microscope. The greatest biodiversity on land is in the top few inches of the soil, where organic matter is constantly recycled and reduced to a size and form useful to the carbon fixing plants and the nitrogen fixing bacteria.

Allowing the garden to recycle its own waste in place creates optimal biodiversity - and with that optimal soil fertility and water holding capacity. Organic gardening is neither time consuming nor expensive.

We often mulch for a single purpose, such as to suppress weeds, prevent water evaporation from the soil, or for aesthetic reasons, and then look for a

Mulch profile

product that will do the job most effectively. But by focusing on a single objective we miss out on all the other benefits provided by Nature's interwoven web of life. Covering the soil with plastic or landscape fabric may prevent some weed seeds from germinating, but it also interrupts the movement of water and air, and deprives the soil organisms of their source of carbohydrates - the recycling organic matter. By "solving" a single problem we have reduced soil biodiversity, soil fertility, soil water holding capacity, and ultimately plant health.

However, when we think of mulching as "feeding the soil dwelling organisms" it all becomes very simple. Our job now is to ensure that these organisms receive the best nutrition possible. The best food for the lawn ecosystem is grass clippings. The best food for a tree or shrub ecosystem is its own discarded leaves and branches. Even in the forest the soil is not smothered in bark! The rest we leave to Nature, which elegantly solves multiple problems with a single solution - providing the ideal food to the soil also protects the soil from compaction, prevents water evaporation, suppresses weed germination, increases soil fertility, increases the soil water holding capacity, increases the soil air supply, and increases plant and ecosystem health.

The earth will be on its way to recovery when the quality of the mulch becomes a status symbol among gardeners.

Mite feeding on a dead leaf

Fertilizing

If we return all the leaves, trimmings and grass clippings to the soil and work to increase soil biodiversity, the fertility of the soil will naturally become more balanced.

Organic fertilizers such as fish and kelp meal, and rock dusts such as basalt, granite and glacial moraine dust can be applied without a soil nutrient analysis because they contain a wide spectrum of nutrients in non-toxic quantities. They are perfect during the transition to organic practices, but seldom required in the long run.

There is no need to worry about "correcting the pH" and "feeding the plants". This happens automatically when we manage our gardens as ecosystems.

Creating deserts

Most synthetic substances - pesticides as well as fertilizers - are poisonous to the soil dwelling organisms. In our desire to "feed" our plants, or to rid them of a particularly troublesome "pest," we kill thousands upon thousands of other animals and microbes, depleting the ecosystem of its biodiversity and resilience. With the depletion of nitrogen fixing bacteria, mycorrhizal fungi and their whole natural support system plants become dependent on chemical inputs.

In time the soil becomes lifeless, hard and cracked, prone to erosion, and unable to support the needs of plants. We call this "desertification". Much of our land base has already become desertified through agricultural and forestry practices that ignore the needs and interdependency of plants and soil dwelling organisms.

Soil testing

In time, organic gardening restores and maintains a healthy nutrient balance in the soil.

For home gardeners, therefore, the most important indicators of soil health are mulch, moisture and microbes.

The mulch must be appropriate for the ecosystem and properly stratified, with a coarse litter layer on top, the finer humus particles incorporating into the soil below.

While the surface of the coarse litter layer may be dry, below it the mulch should be "moist like a wrung out sponge" - exactly the same conditions we are trying to achieve in our compost because this is the ideal moisture environment for microbes.

Finally, it needs to be teeming with life. The upper few inches of the soil, which include the mulch layer, are habitat for the greatest biodiversity on land. Most of the organisms are too small to be seen without a microscope, but many insects and even some fungal strands can be seen with the bare eye or a simple magnifying glass. The greater the diversity, the better.

If we take care of this, Nature takes care of everything else.

In situations such as commercial agriculture or golf course maintenance a more in-depth soil analysis may be required, and the results interpreted by a qualified organic land care professional.

Increasing microbial diversity

Although we can't see them, microbes play an important role in the lives of our plants. The easiest way to maximize microbial diversity is to allow all fallen leaves and branches to recycle back into the soil. But not all gardens have been maintained with such insight. All too often the populations of plant allies have been severely impacted by the use of pesticides or synthetic fertilizers, and then we need to replenish or even re-establish them. Compost and compost tea provide a great diversity of microbes and can be prepared from local materials without great expense. Specific microbial species, such as fermenting microorganisms and mycorrhizal fungi can be purchased in their dormant state and applied as needed.

Compost

Nature mulches – composting is a human invention.

A compost pile is constructed very deliberately as a breeding ground for microbes. We alternate layers of carbon rich and nitrogen rich materials, add a few layers of twigs for aeration, and then provide just enough water so it feels like a wrung out sponge. This provides food, water and habitat for countless organisms, whose populations explode under these ideal conditions.

Well aerated, mature compost contains an incredible diversity of microbes, together with the complex organic compounds created in this microbial feeding frenzy. It also provides a balanced source of nutrients for plants and the soil dwelling organisms.

Compost is an invaluable source of microbes and nutrients when we need to restore soil biodiversity in a chemically managed garden. We can work it directly into the soil as we establish a new planting bed, or simply add it to the soil surface. The more the better, and then we simply protect it with leaf mulch and let Nature do the rest.

Many gardeners make themselves a lot of work by raking up all the leaves, composting them and returning them back to the soil as mulch. This is not only unnecessary but also unfortunate, as it destroys the soil's natural protection, and habitat and food for countless soil dwelling organisms. While compost can kick-start the process, in the long run soil biodiversity will be greater if we leave Nature alone.

By all means, compost the kitchen scraps and any "extras", such as the leaves and branches raked off the patio. Then use your "black gold" as a supplement where it is most needed, and always defer to Nature's wisdom.

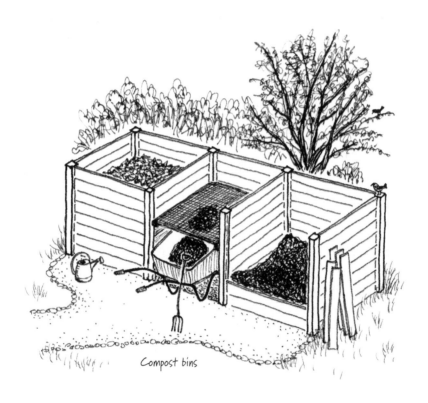

Compost bins

Compost tea

In the gardening environment, the term "tea" is used for many different kinds of brews, such as manure tea, comfrey tea and stinging nettle tea. These kinds of teas are usually simple extracts of nutrients and other organic substances. Sometimes they are allowed to ferment for a few days and then also become a source of fermenting microbes.

Compost tea, however, is deliberately brewed for a specific purpose – to extract and further multiply the microbes present in a small amount of compost. Therefore it is very important to use only high quality mature compost! Anaerobic, foul smelling "compost" contains the wrong kinds of microbes that can actually kill your plants or negatively impact soil biodiversity.

To make compost tea, a few handfuls of compost are added to a special compost tea brewer filled with non-chlorinated water, together with small amounts of microbe food such as un-sulfured molasses, rock dust, kelp meal and sea minerals. Finally, a constant stream of air is injected into the brewer to ensure a sufficient oxygen supply to the microbes. After a couple of days the surface of the brew will be frothy and the tea is ready to be used immediately.

Where compost is in short supply, compost tea is a great alternative for inoculating the soil with microbes. Additionally, the tea can be sprayed onto plant leaf surfaces, helping to protect plants from plant-feeding microbes.

Compost tea is neither a fertilizer nor a pesticide, but a microbial inoculant designed to increase biodiversity in the soil and on plant surfaces. Just as it is important to start with high quality compost, it is equally important to keep the brew well aerated. Compost tea brewers are specially designed to minimize anaerobic pockets, where the wrong kinds of microbes can multiply. As an added measure of caution one can add a few tablespoons of beneficial fermenting microbes, which generally out-compete the pathogens in low oxygen environments.

Finally, it is important to use the finished compost tea immediately, as the brew becomes anaerobic within hours.

Commercial compost tea brewers can be pricey, but many home gardeners report great success with a simple home-made brewer made from a five gallon bucket, an aquarium pump and air tubing.

Organic gardening does not rely on products and compost tea is no exception. It is useful under some circumstances, but certainly not necessary.

Fermenting microbes

Those who make their own sourdough bread or wine already know about fermenting microbes such as lactic acid bacteria and yeasts. We can even make our own sourdough starter by capturing the wild microbes that are present everywhere in our environment, including the air.

Fermenting microbes are often referred to as facultative anaerobes because they can live at normal oxygen concentrations, in completely anaerobic environments, and everywhere in between.

They occupy a very unique niche in the ecology and produce many important products that benefit the whole soil based web of life, such as vitamins, antioxidants, hormones, enzymes, lactic acid, alcohol and antibiotics.

Fermenting microorganisms are plentiful in leaf litter, hence the typical brewery-type odour of leaf mould. They can also be purchased as "EM", "Efficient Microorganisms", "Biosa" and others. They can be sprayed onto the soil or directly onto plant surfaces, with great benefit to plant and ecosystem health. Fermenting microorganisms are widely used in some Asian countries, but not yet well known in other parts of the world.

Healthy Lawns

Lawns are blamed for all kinds of environmental problems, from pesticide use, to wasteful use of water and even for the moss that grows in shaded lawns. But these are not faults of the lawn.

All of them are the result of unfortunate choices: situating the lawn in the wrong light conditions, and treating it like a synthetic environment.

Taking care of the lawn is easy if we think of it as an ecosystem:

Provide appropriate light conditions - situate the lawn in full sun. Remember that the natural overstorey of grasslands is the sky! Mow as high as possible while preserving the lawn's ability to support traffic. Just like trees, grasses preserve the delicate balance between leaf mass (photosynthetic capacity) and root mass (water and nutrient uptake ability). Taller grass results in deeper roots with improved drought tolerance, nutrient uptake, and lawn health in general. This reduces the need for fertilizing and irrigation.

Feed the soil dwelling organisms - always leave the clippings, they are the equivalent to mulch in a garden bed. Never use synthetic fertilizers, which are highly toxic to the microbes. If the lawn needs a nutrient boost during the transition, use an organic fertilizer such as kelp or fish meal, or rock dusts such as basalt, granite or glacial moraine dust. These can be applied without a soil nutrient analysis. This eliminates the need for regular fertilizing and liming.

Increase soil biodiversity by applying mycorrhizal fungi or fermenting microorganisms, and by topdressing with compost or applying compost tea. In the long run this won't be necessary, but it is essential during the transition from conventional to organic practices. The increased fungal populations

...continued

reduce thatch to ideal conditions, just enough to protect the grass crowns from traffic injury. This eliminates the need for de-thatching.

Provide sufficient water for optimal ecosystem health. With a reliable food source (grass clippings), and the occasional deep watering, the increased microbial populations will begin to re-structure the soil. As they rearrange the soil particles to build themselves homes they create the ideal mix of soil pores to increase the soil's water holding capacity, and provide sufficient air for themselves and for plant roots. Over time, this eliminates the need for aerating and greatly reduces - or even eliminates - the need for irrigation.

And what about weeds? Turf grasses were selected for their aggressiveness, their ability to form dense mats and compete with other species. A healthy, biodiverse lawn will have very few weeds, and chances are they won't even be noticeable.

Weeds only flourish in a lawn when the growing conditions are unsuitable for the lawn. This is always the case in low light conditions, where the only solution is to remove the source of shade, or grow something other than lawn. Weeds can also become established when the soil nutrient balance has been impaired due to regular application of synthetic fertilizers and lime. If - in spite of all the good organic management - the weed populations do not diminish, it's time to call in an organic land care professional with advanced education in soil and lawn management.

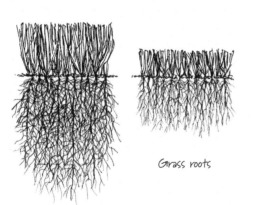

Grass roots

Mycorrhizal fungi

Mycorrhizal fungi are so important to plants that all but 2 plant families are known to form associations with them. Consequently they are prolific in the environment.

However, in some situations their populations are severely depressed or completely lacking, such as in compacted or water-logged soil, "manufactured" topsoil, peat based growing media and soil repeatedly treated with pesticides or synthetic fertilizers. Even tilling will sever the fungal strands and repress fungal populations.

Mycorrhizal fungi can be re-introduced by incorporating them into the top few inches of the soil. A few handfuls of forest or natural grassland soil will do, but the spores can also be purchased. Compost is not a source of mycorrhizal fungi because they can only live in association with the roots of living plants and do not multiply in compost.

In cases where a new garden is planted in imported "manufactured" topsoil it is highly advisable to add mycorrhizal fungi to the planting holes. Plant propagators do not commonly add these fungi to their growing media, nor are they guaranteed to be present in the imported soil. Without these important allies plants are unable to access the water-insoluble phosphorus in the soil, and are also much more prone to drought stress.

Providing sufficient water for ecosystem health

Like all living beings, plants require water – and they require heat to germinate from seed, produce flowers, and mature their fruits. In Mother Nature's garden, heat and plenty of water create ideal conditions for the immense abundance of the tropical rainforests. The same heat without water creates deserts, but even there the occasional rain results in an overnight transformation as dormant seeds germinate and plants rush to complete their life cycle while water is available. Here on the West Coast of Canada most of the rain falls in the winter, and little in the summer. So the greatest show of flowers is in the spring, with plants receding underground and going dormant to reduce their exposure to the summer drought. Our native Garry Oak meadows look brown and unkempt during the summer.

The plants in our food and ornamental gardens, however, come from all areas of the world. For the most part they require the high temperatures of summer to flower and fruit, and with rising temperatures their water requirements also rise.

Our role then is to ensure our gardens have sufficient water. If we have chosen plants that are not adapted to local precipitation patterns we need to irrigate them.

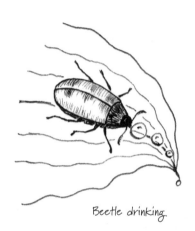

Beetle drinking

Equally important and usually overlooked is the need to ensure that all the organisms in the soil have enough water! After all they are the ones who feed and protect our plants, and they are the ones who increase the water holding capacity of the soil itself. And in Mother Nature's garden the soil is the greatest water reservoir.

Withholding water from our gardens is exactly the wrong answer as we are becoming concerned about dwindling water supplies. It creates a downward spiral of decline, decreasing biodiversity in the soil, reducing the health of our plants and reducing the amount of water our soils can store. Instead we need to work to increase biodiversity both above and below ground. We must beware of the single cause - single effect mentality, and manage our gardens as ecosystems.

Drip irrigation

Currently, the politically correct way to reduce water use in landscapes is through drip irrigation - delivering water directly to plant roots and not "wasting" it on the rest of the soil. This is a prime example of single cause - single effect thinking.

Our garden is not a mere plant collection, but a complex ecosystem - a single interconnected organism - that needs to be managed as a whole. Plants derive their food and countless other vital organic substances from the activity of the soil dwelling organisms. Without them, they will "starve" and become sick. Sick plants become food for plant-feeding insects and microbes.

Drip irrigation was developed for situations where plants derive their nutrition entirely from fertilizers and where their root zone is restricted to a known soil volume, such as in container plant production, or food production in arid climates. Typically those plants are grown in sterile growing media or otherwise lifeless soil. For the most part these are short-term situations, where the plants are harvested at the end of their growing season, or sold and transplanted into the environment. There is no opportunity or intention to develop a functioning soil ecosystem.

In perennial landscapes, drip irrigation is not only unsuitable, it's environmentally irresponsible. Land-based ecosystems have evolved with overhead water. Soil dwelling insects and other animals depend on little pockets of water in the coarse litter layer, and microbial populations will dwindle and become imbalanced without sufficient moisture. A simple rule of thumb is to ensure that the plants don't wilt and the mulch below the litter layer remains "moist as a wrung out sponge". The greater the water holding capacity of the soil, the less supplemental irrigation is required.

Creating health

The buzzword in gardening and agricultural circles these days is "integrated pest management" (IPM). Pest management is nothing more than symptom management - because the real cause of plant disease is nutrient deficiency, not the presence of plant feeding insects or microbes. Killing the insects will not make the plants healthy - plant disease is not a pesticide deficiency.

Worldwide, billions of pounds of pesticides are used every year in an effort to combat plant enemies. Pest management is a warfare approach, health management is a welfare approach. Pest management decreases biodiversity, health management increases biodiversity. Pest management sends the ecosystem on a downward spiral towards ill health and death, health management creates abundance and health for all.

Health management is easy when we manage our gardens, forests and agricultural fields as ecosystems.

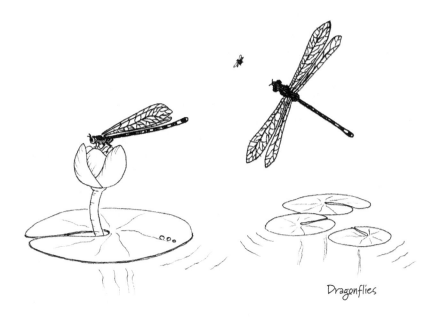

Dragonflies

The essence of organic gardening

And that is it - the essence of organic gardening. We call it organic gardening, because it acknowledges and supports the wholeness of Nature, the interconnectedness of all life.

The beauty of organic gardening is that it allows each of us to make a contribution that benefits the whole. We may think that our actions are insignificant, but every little piece of earth whose biological function has been maintained or repaired adds to the health of the environment overall.

This is important in cities where the natural environment has been virtually destroyed by human activities. And it is also important in the country, where conventional agricultural and forestry practices have severely impacted the natural biodiversity, and reduced the capacity of the soil to support life.

To repair and protect our planet's biodiversity we need to restore and maintain year-round food and habitat for all the earth's creatures.

May your garden be a source of health and abundance!

Heide

Resources

Resources

Books
Heide Hermary, *Working with Nature – Shifting Paradigms*
An in-depth, fully referenced exploration of the science and practice of organic
horticulture. Available from Gaia College:
www.gaiacollege.ca/public/books_&_videos/books/Shifting_Paradigms.php

Education in Organic Horticulture for Professionals and Home Gardeners
Gaia College
www.gaiacollege.ca/

Organic Master Gardener Program
Society for Organic Urban Land Care
www.organiclandcare.org/master gardeners/index.php
Gaia College
www.gaiacollege.ca/public/programs/gardener/index.php

Organic Land Care Standard
Society for Organic Urban Land Care
www.organiclandcare.org/standards/index.php

Organic Certification of Landscape Professionals
Society for Organic Urban Land Care
www.organiclandcare.org/certification/index.php

Certified Organic Professionals
Society for Organic Urban Land Care
www.organiclandcare.org/members/professionals.php

Products for Organic Gardeners
The Organic Gardener's Pantry
www.gardenerspantry.ca

Notes

Lightning Source UK Ltd.
Milton Keynes UK
UKOW07f1825140517

301185UK00018B/464/P